The Olive Press of Affliction

Crushing Season Field Guide

By

Tammy Toney-Butler

Dedication

First, God deserves all the glory and praise in my life. I am nothing without His grace and mercy. I was dead, a shell of a person, until He saw fit to set me free, transform my mind and body, and make me a new creature in Christ. This book is a Holy Spirit-inspired download, written as I embraced my new identity in Christ Jesus and fully stepped into the call

God placed on my life as a Healing Evangelist. It is His masterpiece, and as you read it, please see Him as the author and not me.

Next, I want to thank David, my husband, who stayed with me and showed me what real love was about. A love that embraced the messy believed in my causes and steadied my troubled soul. A love that refused to quit on me when I was caught in an emotional flashback and full of the residue of trauma, dressed in shame-soaked, icky garments full of holes. David offered no judgment, just praise and unconditional love, providing hope that a girl like me, broken, could be worthy of love and sustain it. David empowered me to become the real me and supported me financially until I broke free of the past, and into all God purposed me to become as a warrior for His Kingdom.

Additionally, David's parents are Russ and Seda. Parents who loved me despite my messiness and showed me what it means to be part of a family. Always in my corner, full of unconditional praise and encouragement. Seda, always dressing me for every occasion, and most of all for giving life to their son, David.

To my mother, Dianne, I give thanks. A few weeks before she died, after we prayed, she permitted me to discuss our life, unfiltered, if it would save another family from being destroyed by generational trauma—a mother who made choices based on survival from a trauma-soaked lens—a mother whom I loved dearly despite her failure to mother me as I deserved. A mother who I know now is in heaven, with my baby sister Anita, and would be so proud of the woman I have become in Christ

Jesus. My mother never stopped praising Jesus.

Now, to my father, Marcel, who never really survived Vietnam, and struggled with addiction, coping through alcoholism, and serving through his hidden pain, and helping many as a police officer. A father who lost his battle with complex PTSD suffered in silence until he died with a self-inflicted gunshot wound (suicide) when I was age fifteen, and we buried him on Father's Day. Please reach out for help to all those suffering in silence. The world is a much better place with you in it. A daughter always longs for her father, even if he cannot be one. I loved my dad despite his not being able to parent me as I deserved. I know he would have been proud of me. I was proud of him despite his messiness.

Next, to my baby sister, Anita, who went home to

be with the Lord in 2025. She suffered much but loved much. She was my encourager, and despite our being apart for most of her life, separated by lost promises and broken environments, my love for her never ceased, as did my love for my other siblings. Trauma destroyed my family, and as I journey to keep it from destroying yours, I carry Anita with me. She was strong, despite her body failing her in the aftermath of trauma and coping through various addictions. She was homeless at times, trafficked as a child and adult, had an arrest record, and never spoke of all she endured. As they amputated lower limb by lower limb due to vascular issues, she was in and out of the hospital, and through it all, she remained devoted to and praising the Lord Jesus. I love you, Anita. I will see you again.

Furthermore, to all my brothers and sisters in Christ, I would be nothing without your prayers and love. United, we are stronger. We must be the Light!

Now, to every educator (schoolteacher, principal) who poured into me as a child and influenced my path. You know who you are, and I owe you so much that words could never convey!

Finally, to all the "thrivers" and "overcomers" who have made it and are sowing those seeds of hope. Keep it up, for the harvest is great, and the laborers are few. Keep shining your Light and stay strong as we navigate the darkness of this world. Find your voice and use it! In all things give thanks and pray without ceasing.

Table of Contents

DEDICATION 2
INTRODUCTION 15
OLIVE OIL MILLING 25
SCRIPTURES FOR DIVINE STRENGTH . 43
- Isaiah 40:31 43
- Philippians 4:13 44
- Psalm 46:1-2 44
- Ephesians 6:10-20 45
- 2 Corinthians 12:9 49
- Nehemiah 8:10 50
- Deuteronomy 31:6 51
- 2 Timothy 1:7 51

SCRIPTURES FOR ENCOURAGEMENT 52
- Isaiah 41:10 52
- Romans 8:37-39 53
- Joshua 1:9 54
- 1 Corinthians 10:12-14 55
- Psalm 91 56

ABOUT THE AUTHOR 61
REFLECTIVE SPACES MINISTRY, CORP
.... 67
NOTE FROM THE AUTHOR 74

SOW A SEED: DONATE............................78

CONTACT INFORMATION........................79

HOTLINE SUPPORT..................................82

NURSES UNITED AGAINST HUMAN TRAFFICKING, PA......................................85

Sinner's Prayer to be Saved *88*

Introduction

In the "olive press," a place of crushing, one can either embrace it or run from it. Jesus, in the Garden of Gethsemane, which means "oil press" in Hebrew,[1] was praying because He was sad and troubled in spirit, carrying a heavy burden

---

[1] https://biblehub.com/topical/o/olive_presses_and_winepresses.htm

only He could bear, the Cross; the weight of it all was crushing.[2]

We see this in Matthew 26:38, where Jesus said to Peter and the two sons of Zebedee, *"My heart is so heavy with grief, I feel as if I am dying. Wait here and stay awake with me."* We see in verse 39, Jesus falling to the ground and praying, *"My Father, if it is possible, don't make me drink*

---

[2] Healing Is Your Portion: A Disciple's Guide to Divine Healing, 2026, Toney-Butler, Chapter 4, pg. 59, Healing Is Your Portion Series on Divine Healing

from this cup. But do what you want, not what I want."[3]

How many of you have fallen to the ground, curled up on the floor, cried, under the weight of it all, been crushed in spirit, and screamed out to God?

How many of you have wanted to run away from the storm you're facing, or need to face, to break free of an abusive relationship

---

[3] Matthew 26: 36-46 (ERV, 2006 Bible League International, BibleGateway.com)

that no longer serves you or your children?

Continuing in this passage of scripture in Matthew 26, we see Jesus praying for strength and God's will to be done, *"My Father, if I must do this and it is not possible for me to escape it, then I pray that what you want will be done."*[4] Jesus knew His Kingdom purpose, why He was on earth, and what He must do to save us all.

---

[4] Matthew 26: 36-46 (ERV, 2006 Bible League International, BibleGateway.com)

Jesus made a choice to drink from the cup (spiritual suffering), carry out Father's will, and go through the Cross (spiritual olive press of tremendous suffering), to become the door[5] through which we all can gain access to eternal life, salvation through the belief in Him, and Him alone. Through His suffering work on Calvary, we gained the "Anointing oil of His Presence, the Holy Spirit, the Promise." He became

---

[5] John 10: 9-16 (NKJV)

the very oil in which we anoint others spiritually when we encounter them—a spiritual transfer of eternal life for all who believe.[6] In the New Testament, the oil acts as a visible remembrance of the intangible Holy Spirit, who empowers, heals, restores, redeems, and has become the Light for the world.[7]

---

[6] Healing Is Your Portion: A Disciple's Guide to Divine Healing, 2026, Toney-Butler, Chapter 4, pg. 59, Healing Is Your Portion Series on Divine Healing

[7] Matthew 5:14-16 (New International Version)

You see, Jesus had a choice in the garden: would he run away from His destiny, His purpose, God's will, or surrender, obey, and run towards it, suffering and all. He could have at any time escaped the Cross, but He chose to give up His worldly life so that He could become everlasting life for us all.

Adam and Eve had a choice to make in the garden[8] (soul), Jesus had a choice to

---

[8] Genesis 3: 1-22 (NIV), Genesis 2 (NIV)

make in the garden (soul), and you have an inner choice (soul) to make today in your "spiritual garden of affliction."[9] Remember, you are spirit, live in a body, and possess a soul (mind, will, emotions).[10] The devil can wreak havoc on your soul if you let him. You must take back control over your soul, give no place to the devil, and hear and see

---

[9]https://www.theyoungcatholicwoman.com/archivescollection/cultivating-a-garden-of-growth-an-analogy-for-suffering

[10] https://www.rhema.org/index.php?option=com_content&view=article&id=2614:the-three-parts-of-man&catid=262&Itemid=858

clearly during this season of testing.

During a season of testing, you can choose to have it end quickly by giving in, going against God's will, or you can fight the good fight of faith Paul talks about in 1 Timothy 6:12, and refuse to give in and partner with the devil's deception.[11]

What will you choose? Who will you obey? What voice will you listen to? What cup will you drink from? Will

---

[11] 1 Timothy 6:12 (KJV)

you let go of the past (sinful nature, disobedience, rebellion, trauma, unforgiveness, bitterness, anger, resentment), and step into who God has purposed you to be as an ambassador for the Kingdom of God?

Will you surrender your will for His? Will you allow your inner man (soul) to be healed? Will you remove yourself from relationships and environments that only weigh you down, silence your voice, keep you bound, or will you embrace the uncomfortable unknown and step towards freedom?

Olive Oil Milling

The olive milling process, the same for thousands of years, involves harvesting, cleaning, crushing, malaxing, pressing, bottling, and storage.[12] The harvest date is based on the fruit's maturity and the desired outcome or taste.

---

[12] Florida Olive Council, 2018, https://www.floridaolive.org/services/olive-milling/#:~:text=Crushing:%20After%20fruit%20is%20cleaned,from%20heat%2C%20light%20and%20oxygen.

The olive miller is skilled in knowing just when the fruit needs to come off the tree. A good miller will design the mill to accommodate (shelter) the fruit. More mature fruit with higher water content may require different tools to be used during the crushing process.

The cleaning process is critical for removing foreign debris that could contaminate the fruit, and for preserving oil quality. After a thorough cleansing, the fruit must be crushed using old-style granite crushing stones or more modern methods.

Next, the malaxing (kneading) process involves stirring, and when applying the heat, ensuring the temperature is carefully controlled. Cold extraction methods are used to ensure the temperature is maintained at a lower level so as not to damage (preserve) the unique, character, and quality of the olive.[13] A breaking down of cells occurs during this step, so the oil molecule can be released.

After malaxing (gentle mixing) loosens the oil from the pulp, the mixture is subjected to a pressure process that separates the oil from the flesh, pit, and water, making up the pulp

---

[13] Big Horn Olive oil, https://bhooc.com/blogs/articles/stone-mills-mediterranean-olive-oil-traditions#:~:text=Stone%20mills%20operate%20by%20crushing,further%20protect%20the%20oil's%20freshness.

mixture.[14] Only then is the oil ready to be bottled, stored, and made ready for human consumption.

People are a lot like olives, during seasons of crushing, those fiery furnace seasons,[15] we can feel as if we are being broken, instead of becoming. Becoming like Christ, in character, with a renewed

---

[14] Florida Olive Council, 2018, https://www.floridaolive.org/services/olive-milling/#:~:text=Crushing:%20After%20fruit%20is%20cleaned,from%20heat%2C%20light%20and%20oxygen.
[15] Daniel 3: 16-28 (KJV, NIV)

heart and mind. You see, when you pray to be more like Jesus, you must go through a crushing season of testing.[16] A season where you let go of the world, seek God, and yield to His will for your life instead of your own. Those Garden moments, where you must decide. Will you follow God, or the world?

If you follow the world, the pressure may be less, and often is, but what will you

---

[16] Matthew 4: 1-11 (NIV)

produce? Will enough oil be made ready for your lamp like the bridesmaids, or will you be found lacking and get shut out of the bridal chamber?[17] A question you must ask yourself today is what oil is your life producing? Is it pure, uncontaminated, Christ-like, and able to show others what the Kingdom of God is like, through your behavior? Your actions?

---

[17] Matthew 25: 1-13 (NIV)

Testing seasons, seasons where you cry out to God for a breakthrough, where you declare that God is good no matter what you are facing, and you turn to Him and away from the god of this world, stretch you and grow your faith muscle.[18] A muscle that must be built up before you step into a leadership role within the body (church), or for God to use you at a

---

[18] Rhema.org, Kenneth Hagin Ministries, https://www.rhema.org/index.php?option=com_content&view=article&id=2181:climbing-the-faith-ladder&Itemid=11

greater capacity. He needs to know that you are all in and will not sway with the wind, be double-minded,[19] blown off course, at the first sign of trouble.

Will you praise God in the hallway of affliction, in the desert (wilderness), or just in the promised land? We want to be used by God, but are we willing to endure the Cross as Jesus endured? In Matthew 16: 24-26, we read about Jesus telling His

---

[19] James 1:8 (KJV)

disciples, *"If anyone would come after me, let him deny himself and take up his cross and follow me. For whoever would save his life will lose it, but whoever loses his life for my sake will find it. For what will it profit a man if he gains the whole world and forfeits his soul? Or what shall a man give in return for his soul?"*[20]

Moments of testing, those crushing seasons, are where we become stronger in

---

[20] Matthew 16: 24-26 (ESV, 2025 Text Edition, Crossway, Good News Publishers, BibleGateway.com)

faith, able to endure the hardships that come along with serving God and not the world. Jesus said in John 16:33, *"I have told you these things, so that in me you may have peace. In this world you will have trouble. But take heart! I have overcome the world."*[21]

Just as a good miller knows when to harvest the grapes, when the crushing process is complete after a proper cleansing, how much heat during the malaxing phase

---

[21] John 16:33 (King James Version)

to apply, and when the oil is ready for consumption, God knows when your season of crushing must end. God knows just how much pressure we can sustain, as a part of the refinement process, and will never suffer us to be tempted beyond what we can bear.[22]

In this instant gratification world with which we dwell, this generation finds it challenging to wait on

---

[22] 1 Corinthians 10:13 (KJV, NIV, AMP)

anything, let alone freedom from the refiner's fire.[23] While on the potter's wheel, the clay should not dictate the process, its timing, or what the finished product will look like, but should yield, surrendering to the process and becoming powerless in the shaping, breaking, and re-making.[24]

As survivors of trauma, we like to believe we have power and control now,

---

[23] Malachi 3:2 (KJV), Revelation 3:18 (NIV), James 1: 2-4 (KJV, NIV, AMP)
[24] Isaiah 45: 9 (CSB, CJB)

since we had none as children when all those bad things happened to us. As adults, we swear no one will ever hurt, control, or manipulate us again, only to find ourselves in situations we swore we would never repeat. Situations that render us powerless, manipulated, and under the control of others. Thus, when asked to surrender to this process to become closer to God, we refuse to yield. Yielding, surrendering, however, is what must happen for you to grow in maturity in Christ, build up your faith muscle, and find yourself in a position to be used mightily by God.

God's Word teaches us that He will never leave nor forsake us,[25] and His love endures forever.[26]

Let me be clear, God is not like those men or women who hurt or disappoint you. God is a good Father. A

---
[25] Deuteronomy 31:6 (NIV, KJV, AMP)
[26] Psalm 136 (NIV)

Father who loved us so much He sent His only Begotten Son, Jesus, to die on the Cross, so we could live free from the condemnation of sin and the curse of the law, and have everlasting life.[27] For cursed was anyone who hangeth on a tree (Cross).[28]

I encourage you during this "olive press" season that you surrender to God's leading of your life by way of the Holy Spirit, the Spirit

---

[27] John 3:16 (KJV, NIV, AMP)
[28] Galatians 3:13 (ESV, KJV)

of Jesus, that dwells on the inside of you, and become like the olive. Trust the miller, trust the process, and know this crushing season will not destroy you; instead, it's shaping you, refining your character, and giving you the courage to step out in faith as a unique, jewel,[29] ready to step into all God has purposed for your life. God can use a surrendered, yielded vessel, so become that person. Repent daily. Ask God for

---

[29] Malachi 3:17 (AMPC)

forgiveness because you know you have missed it and draw strength from the scriptures. The Word of God is our go-to during seasons of crushing, pruning, breaking, and remaking.

Let these following pages arm you with God's Truth, strengthen your inner man, and let you know, you are not alone. A field guide for you as you go out into the world, like the early disciples, surrendered, and empowered by the Holy Spirit.

Scriptures for Divine Strength

Isaiah 40:31
King James Version

31 But they that wait upon the Lord shall renew their strength; they shall mount up with wings as eagles; they shall run, and not be weary; and they shall walk, and not faint.

Philippians 4:13
King James Version
13 I can do all things through Christ which strengtheneth me.

Psalm 46:1-2
King James Version
46 God is our refuge and strength, a very present help in trouble. 2 Therefore will not we fear, though the earth be removed, and though the mountains be carried into the midst of the sea;

Ephesians 6:10-20
King James Version

10 Finally, my brethren, be strong in the Lord, and in the power of his might.

11 Put on the whole armour of God, that ye may be able to stand against the wiles of the devil.

12 For we wrestle not against flesh and blood, but against principalities, against powers, against the rulers of the darkness of this world,

against spiritual wickedness in high places.

13 Wherefore take unto you the whole armour of God, that ye may be able to withstand in the evil day, and having done all, to stand.

14 Stand therefore, having your loins girt about with truth, and having on the breastplate of righteousness;

15 And your feet shod with the preparation of the gospel of peace;

16 Above all, taking the shield of faith, wherewith ye shall be able to quench all the fiery darts of the wicked.

17 And take the helmet of salvation, and the sword of the Spirit, which is the word of God:

18 Praying always with all prayer and supplication in

the Spirit, and watching thereunto with all perseverance and supplication for all saints;

19 And for me, that utterance may be given unto me, that I may open my mouth boldly, to make known the mystery of the gospel,

20 For which I am an ambassador in bonds: that therein I may speak boldly, as I ought to speak.

2 Corinthians 12:9
King James Version

9 And he said unto me, My grace is sufficient for thee: for my strength is made perfect in weakness. Most gladly therefore will I rather glory in my infirmities, that the power of Christ may rest upon me.

Nehemiah 8:10
Complete Jewish Bible

10 Then he said to them, "Go, eat rich food, drink sweet drinks, and send portions to those who can't provide for themselves; for today is consecrated to our Lord. Don't be sad, because the joy of Adonai is your strength."

Deuteronomy 31:6
Complete Jewish Bible[30]

6 Be strong, be bold, don't be afraid or frightened of them, for Adonai your God is going with you. He will neither fail you nor abandon you."

2 Timothy 1:7
King James Version

7 For God hath not given us the spirit of fear; but of power, and of love, and of a sound mind.

---

[30] Complete Jewish Bible (CJB), 1998, David H. Stern

Scriptures for Encouragement

Isaiah 41:10
Amplified Bible[31]

'Do not fear [anything], for I am with you; Do not be afraid, for I am your God. I will strengthen you, be assured I will help you; I will certainly take hold of you with My righteous right hand [a hand of justice, of power, of victory, of salvation].'

---

[31] Amplified Bible (AMP), 2015, The Lockman Foundation

Romans 8:37-39
King James Version

37 Nay, in all these things we are more than conquerors through him that loved us.
38 For I am persuaded, that neither death, nor life, nor angels, nor principalities, nor powers, nor things present, nor things to come,
39 Nor height, nor depth, nor any other creature, shall be able to separate us from the love of God, which is in Christ Jesus our Lord.

Joshua 1:9
King James Version[32]

9 Have not I commanded thee? Be strong and of a good courage; be not afraid, neither be thou dismayed: for the Lord thy God is with thee whithersoever thou goest.

---

[32] King James Version (KJV), Public Domain

1 Corinthians 10:12-14
Christian Standard Bible[33]

12 So, whoever thinks he stands must be careful not to fall. 13 No temptation has come upon you except what is common to humanity. But God is faithful; he will not allow you to be tempted beyond what you are able, but with the temptation he will also provide the way out so that you may be able to bear it.

---

[33] Christian Standard Bible (CSB), 2017, Holman Bible Publishers

Psalm 91
King James Version

91 He that dwelleth in the secret place of the most High shall abide under the shadow of the Almighty.

2 I will say of the Lord, He is my refuge and my fortress: my God; in him will I trust.

3 Surely he shall deliver thee from the snare of the fowler, and from the noisome pestilence.

4 He shall cover thee with his feathers, and under his wings shalt thou trust: his truth shall be thy shield and buckler.

5 Thou shalt not be afraid for the terror by night; nor for the arrow that flieth by day;

6 Nor for the pestilence that walketh in darkness; nor for the destruction that wasteth at noonday.

7 A thousand shall fall at thy side, and ten thousand at thy right hand; but it shall not come nigh thee.

8 Only with thine eyes shalt thou behold and see the reward of the wicked.

9 Because thou hast made the Lord, which is my refuge, even the most High, thy habitation;

10 There shall no evil befall thee, neither shall any

plague come nigh thy dwelling.

11 For he shall give his angels charge over thee, to keep thee in all thy ways.

12 They shall bear thee up in their hands, lest thou dash thy foot against a stone.

13 Thou shalt tread upon the lion and adder: the young lion and the dragon shalt thou trample under feet.

14 Because he hath set his love upon me, therefore will I deliver him: I will set him on high, because he hath known my name.

15 He shall call upon me, and I will answer him: I will be with him in trouble; I will deliver him, and honour him.

16 With long life will I satisfy him, and shew him my salvation.

About the Author

Reflective Spaces Ministry, Corp, is a 501(c)(3) non-profit founded in 2021 by Tammy Toney-Butler, a former emergency department nurse and sexual assault nurse examiner.
Following the whisper of the Holy Spirit, she and her husband relocated to Lee County, Florida. They purchased a ten-acre parcel

of land to begin a trauma-focused, healing ministry.

Tammy, a Healing Evangelist, can be found on the streets, going after the ones. Tammy's lived experience provides a unique teaching style and trauma-focused lens perspective, offering survivors environments conducive to healing mind, body, and spirit.

Tammy Toney-Butler, as a teenager, survived the loss

of her father to suicide. She overcame being a victim of child sex trafficking and coping with the aftermath of trauma through various addictions through her faith in the Lord Jesus and is a powerful testimony of faith in action.

In 2023, Reflective Hour with Tammy Toney-Butler was launched in podcast and YouTube formats as a platform for transformational healing in Christ. The Reflective Spaces Ministry podcast was launched in podcast and YouTube formats in 2024.

Tammy is outspoken in her mission to provide a trauma-responsive pulpit and a compassionate, merciful lens through which one offers pastoral support. Love is her focus because the love of Jesus Christ heals all wounds, delivers, and transforms.

Tammy has become the mouthpiece for God's message of hope and healing worldwide. She is a published author whose works have been featured in the National Library of Medicine, Congress.gov, textbooks, and several professional journals.

Her memoir and healing devotional with journal pages are available on Amazon and Kindle.

Tammy has spoken at the United Nations, American Nurses Association (ANA) General Assembly, ANA New York, ANA Georgia,

ANA Vermont, and has been a guest on network television.

From the ranch to the pulpit, from the trailer park to the assembly hall, God has moved mightily in Tammy's life, and the Lord Jesus Christ gets all the credit and honor for her transformation and restoration.

Reflective Spaces Ministry, Corp

Reflective Spaces Ministry, Corp, is a 501(c)(3) non-profit founded in 2021 by Tammy Toney-Butler, a former emergency department nurse and sexual assault nurse examiner. Following the Holy Spirit's whisper, she and her husband, David, relocated to Lee County, Florida. They purchased a ten-acre parcel of land to begin a trauma-focused, healing ministry.

The mission of Reflective Spaces Ministry is to provide reflective spaces for transformational healing and total restoration in a faith-filled environment for survivors of human trafficking, sexual violence, domestic violence, and childhood adversity to thrive. In 2025, our Founder, Tammy Toney-Butler, on her journey to wholeness, had an awakening as to the fundamental mission of Reflective Spaces Ministry.

Our goal is to show the heart of Christ to all we encounter, empowering and enabling them with the strength and courage required to look inward, reflect on the past adversities faced, and live transformed lives despite it. A reflective space within one's own heart, full of strength, power, and courage to face the dark, refuse to let it break them, and instead, process and overcome it one layer at a time. Bringing them to wholeness, physically, mentally, spiritually, and financially.

Consider donating to our direct survivor assistance programs, including day programs such as respite retreats for spiritual renewal through nature, as well as free healing ministry services. The team believes in empowering every survivor with a safe retreat experience in a private setting while they process the dark and transition into the Light. Survivor empowerment is vital to recovery; assisting survivors/thrivers with transportation and living expenses as they transition on their healing journey is vital to long-term success.

Reflective Spaces Ministry assesses and meets them where they are on their healing journey, whatever that looks like for their unique situation. Finding gaps in existing services and bridging those ensures an overall positive transitional health experience. Overcoming barriers to care and supplying Maslow's Basic Hierarchy of Needs ensures that youth transitioning into adulthood and vulnerable adults will not be left behind. "Throw-Away" youth are vulnerable to trafficking and exploitation; thus, wraparound support is needed to bridge gaps and provide pathways for success.

Positive mentoring, role modeling, and empowerment are essential for this generation of young warriors to tap into their hidden purpose and become all God has called them to be in this stage of their lives. Positive childhood experiences (PACES), such as a day retreat at A&K Ranch, can help mitigate the effects of adverse childhood experiences (ACES). Empowering "thrivers" with resources and choices as they journey to wholeness is a mission worthy of your financial support.

Note from the Author

As a survivor of child sex trafficking and loss of father to suicide as a teenager, I know trauma and loss all too well. Our ministry, Reflective Spaces Ministry, focuses on hope and healing, one layer at a time. Through quiet reflection and inner work, one can achieve wholeness through faith in the Lord Jesus Christ, as I have done by His grace and mercy on my life.

As a Healing Evangelist, my heart is for the lost, broken, wounded, and those coping with trauma through various addictions. Love heals and transforms, as evidenced by our Lord and Savior, Jesus Christ. My goal, His goal, is to empower, inform, and equip with the tools needed to thrive as maturity through faith increases, and deliverance is possible. I am not just interested in getting them out of Egypt but getting Egypt out of them. A renewed mind is possible, with ultimate healing in four key areas of fitness: spiritual, mental, physical, and financial. Achieving wholeness is possible if one puts the work in. Trauma destroyed my family, and I am on a mission to save yours and all those I encounter. Breaking generational patterns of abuse is an essential component of healing, trauma work, and a focus of our ministry. Thank you again for trusting me to deliver a healing message to you by way of His books.

Blessings and Peace,

Tammy Toney-Butler,
Healing Evangelist

Sow A Seed: Donate

Consider SOWING A SEED to further our community outreach and evangelism efforts to spread the Gospel worldwide!
Even if the ninety-nine are safe, we go after the one! Partner with our ministry by clicking on the ministry link below to help us gather the ones into the family of Light.

https://www.reflectivespacesministry.com/

https://www.paypal.com/fundraiser/charity/4406377

https://account.venmo.com/u/Reflectivespacesministry

Contact Information

Tammy Toney-Butler, Reflective Spaces Ministry, Corp, 16295 S. Tamiami Trail, Suite # 133, Fort Myers, FL 33908
info@reflectivespacesministry.com

www.reflectivespacesministry.com

www.reflectivespacespodcast.com

Reflective Hour with Tammy Toney-Butler is available at:
www.reflectivehour.com

You can purchase her book on Amazon Kindle, "When you know, that you know, that you know there is a God."

https://www.amazon.com/stores/Tammy-Toney-Butler/author/B0DC1VXP45?ref=ap_rdr&isDramIntegrated=true&shoppingPortalEnabled=true

About Tammy: https://www.reflectivespacesministry.com/about

Tammy is available to teach and empower women and men as they journey to wholeness through the Light and Love of Christ.

Contact her to book an in-person prophetic healing session, meeting, service, or conference at www.tammytoneybutler.com

Hotline Support

Hotline numbers:
https://www.reflectivespacesministry.com/contact

National Human Trafficking Hotline
1-888-373-7888

Report Human Trafficking in Florida, call 1-855-352-7233
1 (855) FLA-SAFE

Report Human Trafficking in Georgia, call 1-866-363-4842

National Center on Missing and Exploited Children Cyber Tip Line
1-800-THE-LOST
1-800-843-5678

Suicide & Crisis Lifeline
988

National Sexual Assault
Hotline
1-800-656-4673

National Teen Dating
Abuse Hotline
1-866-331-9474

Runaway Hotline
1-800-786-2929

Domestic Violence Hotline
1-800-799-7233

Department of Homeland Security to Report Human Trafficking
1-866-347-2423

Nurses United Against Human Trafficking, PA

Nurses United Against Human Trafficking (NUAHT) was founded in 2020 by two nurses driven to abolish modern-day slavery. Dr. Francine Bono-Neri and Tammy Toney-Butler. NUAHT offers education modules, membership resources, and consulting services for healthcare professionals, by building human trafficking protocols and community response teams.

The mission of NUAHT is to eradicate human trafficking by raising awareness, providing education and resources, and participating in advocacy efforts, all for the hope of emboldening and empowering healthcare professionals, by establishing best practices and standards of care for this vulnerable and invisible population.

For every membership purchased, NUAHT donates to Reflective Spaces Ministry, a direct service provider for survivors of human trafficking, sexual and physical violence, and childhood adversity (trauma). Reflective Spaces Ministry provides all services for free.

Sinner's Prayer to be Saved

Dear Heavenly Father,

I come to you in the Name of Jesus. Your Word says, "The one who comes to Me I will by no means cast out" (John 6:37 NKJV). I know You won't cast me out or turn me away. I know You take me in and I am grateful for You and thank You. You said in Your Word, "Whoever calls on the name of the Lord shall be saved"

(Romans 10:13 NKJV). I am calling on Your Name, now, Oh Lord, and I believe You have saved me, a lost sinner. You also state in Your Word, in Romans 10: 9-10, "If you confess with your mouth the Lord Jesus and believe in your heart that God has raised Him from the dead, you will be saved. For with the heart, one believes unto righteousness, and with the mouth of confession is made unto salvation." I believe Jesus rose from the dead for my justification. I am now reconciled to God. I confess Jesus as My Lord and Savior. Because Your Word says that "with the heart one believes unto righteousness," and I do believe with my heart, I have now become the righteousness of God in Christ (2 Corinthians 5:21). I now know I have been redeemed, restored, saved by the blood of Jesus.

Thank You, Lord Jesus. I praise and honor You and

believe with this prayer and declaration that the Holy Spirit, Your Spirit, lives inside of me, making me fresh, clean, and new. I surrender to God's will for my life, instead of my will. Thank You, God, for giving me the heart and mind of Christ, for washing me clean, and setting me free.

If you prayed this prayer, welcome to the family! Please email us at info@reflectivespacesministry.com to discuss next steps and mail you out resources for your walk as a new Christian.[34]

(Prayer adapted from Kenneth E. Hagin's Laying on of Hands Book, pg. 33, Rhema Bible Church.[35]

---

[34] Healing Is Your Portion Series on Divine Healing by Tammy Toney-Butler, A Healing Trilogy.
https://www.amazon.com/dp/B0GGWFK54F?binding=kindle_edition&ref=dbs_m_mng_rwt_sft_tkin_tpbk&qid=1768464747&sr=1-3

[35] https://www.rhemabiblechurch.com/

www.ingramcontent.com/pod-product-compliance
Lightning Source LLC
Chambersburg PA
CBHW060342050426
42449CB00011B/2815